Show Me the Money

Show Me the Money

Where Did All the Aid and Money Go After Typhoon Yolanda in the Philippines November 2013

GRAHAM MICHAEL BARTON

authorHOUSE®

AuthorHouse™ UK
1663 Liberty Drive
Bloomington, IN 47403 USA
www.authorhouse.co.uk
Phone: 0800.197.4150

© 2014 Graham Michael Barton. All rights reserved.

No part of this book may be reproduced, stored in a retrieval system, or transmitted by any means without the written permission of the author.

Published by AuthorHouse 10/22/2014

ISBN: 978-1-4969-9407-3 (sc)
ISBN: 978-1-4969-9408-0 (e)

Any people depicted in stock imagery provided by Thinkstock are models, and such images are being used for illustrative purposes only. Certain stock imagery © Thinkstock.

This book is printed on acid-free paper.

Because of the dynamic nature of the Internet, any web addresses or links contained in this book may have changed since publication and may no longer be valid. The views expressed in this work are solely those of the author and do not necessarily reflect the views of the publisher, and the publisher hereby disclaims any responsibility for them.

Contents

Arriving 1
Distribution 4
International Rescue 15
Images 18
Job Done in Cebu 22
The Airbase 30
The Shopping Mall Experience 35
Christmas Island 39
New Year's Day 46
Rebuilding 49
Juxtaposition of Circumstances 53
Three Months and Counting 59
What's Next? 62
Tacloban 63

Foreword

This book was put together after the super typhoon Haiyan (also known as Yolanda) tore through a large chunk of the thousands of islands that make up the Philippines in November 2013. Coverage of this tropical cyclone made the world aware of names such as Tacloban, Ormoc, Biliran Province, and Samar. Its immediate destruction was catastrophic, but what took place afterwards was possibly even more damaging to the people of the Philippines and their future.

The international response bordered on magnificent. In contrast, the Philippine government, its political representatives, and its authorities were anything but. We watched in disbelief and horror as they systematically shafted their own people and imagined chaining them to one of the islands that occasionally sinks into the ocean. I won't pretend for a moment that this is a dispassionate or all-encompassing account of the aftermath of Typhoon Yolanda, for I arrived ten days after she did. However, I hope the following chapters will give you this Englishman's overview and direct knowledge explaining why the totally inadequate response to typhoon and other disasters should never be allowed to happen again. There may be apocryphal stories, certainly unbelievable and some perhaps untrue, but where there's smoke, there's fire.

Arriving

The whole vista of the island has shockingly changed. The thick clumps of lush coconut trees have been stripped, as if a giant hand reached down from the heavens, took hold of half a dozen mature trees and plucked them from the earth, and then discarded them willy-nilly. I saw twenty-year-old trees toppled like matchsticks, the roots torn from the earth and exposed to the wind. Nepa huts were flattened, paths were blocked, and corrugated tin roofs were bent and battered so much that it looked like they had been in a car-crushing machine. The frontage on the island looked like a row of teeth after losing in a particularly bruising boxing match—raw gums and teeth missing.

The boat approached the harbour— well, a randomly stacked pile of rocks opposite the shifting sandbar. Any residences in this area were pulverized. Trees had crashed through homes, boats were tossed around, reduced to matchwood, and a small fishing boat managed to find itself atop the gated concrete entranceway to the half-demolished jetty. The fairly imposing residence built by the family who hid President Marcos during World War II looked like somebody took a giant blowtorch to it. The roof had completely vanished, the walls were caved in, doors flattened, windows gone. Finally, Yolanda converted the rocks carried laboriously by hand to form a makeshift seawall into projectiles and fired it at random all over the seafront.

The Pinoy boat passengers were unusually quiet, for if this was the front of the island, what on earth would the rest of it look like? The thought *completely buggered* springs to mind. Nearly every house still standing had visible damage. I saw gaps where some houses just weren't there anymore. The wooden electricity poles and wires were felled, ripping up the only concrete roadway on the island. Wires hung everywhere. There was no fear of electric shock, of course – the shock would have been if the electricity were supplied. Islanders wandered around, shell-shocked, as wire fences rolled into balls were blown across the island like tumbleweed, debris everywhere. Whatever you've seen or heard about the destruction after the storm, multiply it by ten, and you'll have an accurate picture. As I write this a few months post-Yolanda, the scene hasn't changed much. If this book can somehow inform and explain why this tiny islandof Higatangan biliran and many others are still reeling from the tropical cyclone and shame the authorities into doing something, my time and effort will have been worth it. The money earned from this book may also improve the state of things. You see, nothing significant has been done by the authorities to help this island of around three thousand people.

Private aid and personal assistance made contributions initially, but now the question is, Where is the government aid, the rebuilding plan, materials, and most importantly, the money? It's hard for me not to turn this book into a tirade against authorities. But really, come on chaps, get your snouts out of the trough and try to put your people before the shiny new car you want. Bringing these shadowy figures to account is nigh on impossible, and it can be extremely dangerous. Foreigners are completely ignored. However, this time, we raise our voices in righteous indignation and say, "Hey, you thieving bastards, show us the money and where it went." Raised voices, emails, letters, phone calls, and almost any form of communication apart from a loaded pistol have been and will be ignored. I've contacted numerous agencies, authorities, and even the president's office, but I never got a reply, not even a rude or threatening one. They are masters of mute indolence and damn insolence, simply raising their eyebrows with skill honed to perfection. I watched a letter of complaint which I delivered directly to the immigration office by hand get placed into a suggestion box, the contents of which I had been informed was regularly emptied and disposed of in a rubbish bin. It's a tried and tested approach at this office: ignore it or bin it, especially if it's from a foreigner, has no bribe value, or is full of intelligent suggestions that could make life easier for all parties.

Distribution

Distribution of aid in its various forms was and is the vital ingredient for taking maximum advantage of the massive international response to such a disaster. C-130 cargo planes and aircraft carriers from America went to small Filipino communities worldwide, selling sticky rice and cakes and then sending the money back to the Philippines. An operation this size is open to all sorts of errors in a country not known for efficiency and notorious for its inability to control corruption. Helping millions of Filipinos who lost their homes, family members, and possessions was going to be a challenge regardless.

Let's look at the example of a foreigner who retired in Cebu and stayed to help. He formed a motorbike club as sort of small and less perfect Hell's Angels. This mixture of leathery old foreigners and eager young Pinoys banded together and spent their weekends on bike tours. They raised an amazing one million pesos within a few short weeks of Yolanda. With these funds, they purchased a selection of traditional aid goods: rice, noodles, canned goods, matches, and small but effective solar lights. Cebu was on the edge of the area Yolanda damaged, so this man also organized boats and trucks to deliver supplies to the area where the centre of the storm hit. He sent trusted Filipinos ahead of the delivery with pre-printed vouchers to distribute amongst the neediest in a specific area of northern Cebu which had suffered greatly. When he arrived a few days later with the trucks, hundreds of people waited patiently, armed with voucher in their outstretched hands. There were far more people and vouchers than the aid he had to give. What had gone wrong? His trusted Filipinos had not thought ahead as carefully as he did. They had duplicated and printed hundreds more vouchers and sold them to those willing to pay. The whole thing descended into a farce and eventually a fight, as everyone thought they deserved the aid they paid for.

During normal times, distribution of goods or services to over 7,000 islands is difficult, and the reality is that on a day-to-day basis, it's shambolic. There are too many examples of corruption and inefficiency. Call it what you will, but rather than pick at examples, let me relate the experiences I suffered through during the Yolanda disaster. Whilst I was fortunate to be in the United Kingdom when the typhoon struck, my beach resort was right in its path. Approximately 80 per cent of the Emponet Barton Beach Resort, on Higatangan Island, Naval, Biliran, Philippines suffered damage. Amazingly, no lives were lost, but my personal home vanished from the beachfront. To be fair, I had been told it was a dodgy place to build. Native cottages, tables, and seats all vanished too. Oh, yes! A roof was torn off a restaurant virtually intact, and then it was transported and deposited onto the smashed remains of a nearby, somewhat flimsy, church building. It was a strange sight. It was a bizarre act of God for which this confirmed agnostic cannot be held responsible—can he? The locals surely tried to blame me.

There was a sad vista of Emponet Barton Beach Resort as you stood across from the broken, flattened chicken sheds. Surprisingly, no chickens were lost in the storm. I wonder if there's a secret storm shelter. The demolished outdoor kitchen and dining area has two remaining hollow block walls and skeletal roof timber still hanging on precariously. Of course, there is a recovered table and chairs, and the Pinoys insist on eating every meal in this area which cannot be called a dining room by any stretch of the imagination. Roofs are gone and many walls are just piles of rubble on virtually every structure I saw. Everything inside - beds, cabinets, tables has been drenched by the storm. Our impressive front gate was torn from its hinges as if the Hulk ripped it apart. Many of the materials were scattered across the Philippine Sea towards China. I wondered if my oldest son, Alex, who lives and works in Shanghai, China, would stumble across a fisherman who had proudly used a fragmented piece of the Emponet Barton Beach Resort (EBBR) sign repair to his fishing boat. So many of our name boards disappeared that I felt it was a surreal take on a message in a bottle. Suffice it to say, the resort was a mess. However, no lives were lost and just a few almost embarrassing injuries. Despite the comedic stereotype, being hit by a flying coconut can cause serious injury or even death. Similarly, the corrugated tin roofing sheets, driven by the wind, become flat guided missiles that can slice through limbs. Fortunately, none of this happened; only minor wounds were suffered. The complete lack of medical facilities and clean water was more of a risk than minor cuts and abrasions.

Twenty or so families, poor even in Filipino terms, lived on our land in rickety nepa huts after losing their local homes. We didn't charge any rent. Instead, we asked for their help cleaning and tidying the beach one day a month. That was the deal. Come to think of it, by the time we gave the kids - on average, five per family - sweets, provided beer and cigarettes for the men, and more beer and Coke for the ladies, we were probably paying them to live on our land. Yet they desperately needed help - specifically, some of that mythical international aid. In summary, the area suffered total devastation, followed by corruption and mismanagement on a grand scale. Higatangan Island was one of many such unfortunate communities attacked by Typhoon Yolanda. What is the difference between a hurricane and a typhoon? The results are mostly the same if you're in its path, but I believe the typhoon starts over the sea, and a hurricane starts over land. You can always check the dictionary for a boring definition.

So, this was the scene when aid poured into the hub city of Cebu, which was nearest to the disaster area. The supplies then left that island to be distributed by boat, truck, and initially helicopters. That's how the big boys do it, don't they - the governments, international agencies, major charities, and teams of people dedicated to saving lives and giving aid? I'm just a private British citizen who happens to live in the Philippines, so I'm not part of any massive organization's efforts required in this moment of great need. But as I write this a couple months after Yolanda hit, my tiny island of Higatangan should be renamed the

Forgotten Island because of the pathetic trickle of aid. It arrived after getting rifled through and exchanged for out-of-date local goods, repackaged in a plastic bag labelled DSWD (Department of Social Welfare and Development), the Philippine government department supposedly dealing with distribution. The few bags that did survive this process were jealously guarded locally and then handed out to those who voted for that particular official, the one who paid for the most votes but does nothing.

Imagine standing in line, waiting for a large bag of hard dusty rice, chewy noodles, expired tins of sardines, and a box of wet matches. The sun blazes down on you, and your children cry with hunger. You will probably be bypassed in favour of a not-so-needy person just because you did not vote for the so-called right person. The aid piles up in warehouses – believe me, I've seen it. The money generously donated reached the pockets of those who didn't deserve it or need it. If this was just a myth, I would not be writing this book. However, if this disaster is investigated by the international community that responded swiftly, justice would be swift and meted out ruthlessly, but you and I know the world will have moved on to other headlines. Pop stars dying of drug-induced self-inflicted comas will be the topic of conversations. They will wring their hands search their souls, but nothing will change unless small voices of reason and retribution band together and ask questions of the Filipino government, such as: what happened to the tons of aid, international and domestic, where is all that money sent from around the world, and, oh yes, how will you spend the 34 trillion – yes, trillion – pesos you have on loan from the world bank for the purpose of rebuilding the shattered homes and infrastructures of your country?

The people from other countries who come to help after Yolanda should also demand, "Show me the money and the rebuilding program." I can't wait for the resources to get to our island. With that amount of money, everyone should get enough to build a three-story mansion and maybe a new luxury car. Pardon me if you detect a hint of utter disbelief. Just once, I'd like to be proved wrong and see some funds actually go towards rebuilding the devastated communities.

But they just can't resist it, can they? Drugs and medical supplies from abroad arrive by the plane load. What a gift for the corrupt Filipino officials, who spirit it away and quickly replace it with local generic drugs and tablets in the same packaging. Many are out of date or unsuitable. They keep the foreign drugs to sell them at a later date for a maximum profit. Even sterilized syringes designed to immunize children are swapped for locally used ones, which is totally inappropriate and certainly dangerous. I saw a picture on social media of three fat Pinoy Red Cross officials, seemingly praying over a pile of money and aid goods, with the caption "These men are praying for another disaster so they can steal more from us." Indeed, social media platforms have been awash with comments on government corruption before Typhoon Yolanda and now regarding its response to the tropical cyclone.

The facts surrounding this disaster have been simultaneously all too familiar and confusing, starting with why the rest of the world called the storm system Hayian, but the Pinoy called it Yolanda. The logical answer is that the Philippines suffer typhoons from September to February. The first one starts with the letter A - Ada, for example- running until

Z. By the time Yolanda arrived, the island had experience more than twenty typhoons that year. The residents and their leaders should be familiar with the cycle, and dare I say prepared for it. Hindsight tells us that they weren't. After the typhoon warning was given, the Philippine president somewhat petulantly issued evacuation orders, but they were mostly ignored. Where exactly do you evacuate to when you're stuck on a tiny island in an area where the surrounding area of land are in the same boat – or rather, not in a boat, because there are not enough to evacuate everyone. Leadership is not just about issuing orders but providing the means to implement them. As a citizen of the United Kingdom, I cannot possibly see the full picture, and my musings are by very nature selective, revolving around my own experiences. What concerns me is that I don't think anyone else grasps the enormous necessity of dealing effectively with the big picture of such a problem. We cannot always wait and see what the lofty powers that be deign to provide next time – and there will definitely be a next time. My modest suggestion, already implemented in Higatangan Island, is to create a disaster response program. Why not put in place a plan flexible enough to take in large and small communities that need help during the violence of a typhoon? Higatangan has a designated six-person team which covers all aspects of such a disaster situation. Following is a copy of this strategy for your reference. Any officials and authorities are welcome to use it, as it has no copyright. However, I can only hope that it won't be used as toilet paper or utterly ignored.

Disaster Response and Resource Plan for Higatangan Island

Following the Super Typhoon Yolanda in 2013, disaster responses were inadequate, as was access to international and local aid. The small community of over 2,700 people, living in 600 homes that ranged from substantial brick and tile to the traditional nipa huts made of flimsy local materials, was severely affected. In a country of over 7,000 islands, it was inevitable that some communities would be missed or ignored, and this happened to Higatangan Island, Naval, Biliran. It was left up to private individuals to arrange for aid by boat, initially, and then from the Philippine Air Force once helicopters were organized to take on the brunt of the responsibility. It is clear that a plan must be instituted to cope with future disasters in the region, especially typhoons. Politics can unfortunately hinder the situation, rather than help, and therefore must be incorporated with careful consideration. Particularly, the adversarial nature of Philippine politicians must be taken into account. Wherever possible, it is best to use those who can be verified as honest, efficient, and capable of doing the job to which they were elected.

Initial Warning and Information: With a history of typhoons, earthquakes, other storms, and floods, there is a wealth of information available via the Internet, TV, and radio about when these situations are likely to arise. Higatangan has a mobile phone and text message warning service run by the coastguard, not to mention word of mouth. However, electrical power and the Internet are spasmodic. During Yolanda, cell phone signals were lost almost immediately. Because communication is vital, a single communications official must be able to sift through all the reports and inform the appropriate disaster response commander and his or her team. A walkie-talkie able to reach the entire island would be ideal. In the absence of this, young people designated as runners between barangays (villages) could be put in place.

Command Centre: This is preferably centrally located on secure premises, where barangay police are posted in the first stages of disaster response. These preparations complement the existing practices of tying up all the boats, securing all houses, and identifying hazards such as structures with corrugated tin roofs or large trees.

It will be a chaotic time, so a KISS (keep it simple, stupid) approach to the command structure is vital.

DRC (disaster response commander): One or both of the barangay captains, thats the headman or woman or the village,l must be in the command centre to direct operations without leaving the command post.

ADRC (assistant disaster response commander): This person will be fully apprised of all incoming information and actions.

CO (communications official): This person is responsible for collating and disseminating all information and will establish contact with the coastguard, army, navy, air force, local politicians, and any other agencies that can get aid to the island swiftly. This information must be then passed to the DCR.

PL (police leader): This person's responsibilities include quelling any unrest as well as advising, informing, and controlling the public. He or she also protects the command centre and acts as a visual and physical presence of order on the island.

MO (medical officer): The person on the island best qualified to deal with major and minor injuries will gather all medical staff at the medical centre to prepare for incoming patients. This officer will have a designated runner with direct communication to the DRC, who may have to arrange evacuation of serious injury cases. Where possible, all medical supplies must be collected and come under the authority of MO.

RS (reserve official): An individual with flexible skills, who responds swiftly to fill any gaps in the disaster response team as dictated by the situation and authorized by the DRC.

The preceding six individuals must work as a team to manage the disaster response as it unfolds.

DRA (disaster response assistants): These people can be appointed and used where required. For example, the medical officer will need nurses, stretcher-bearers, and runners.

At least every six months, the team should practise the DRR plan. Every year, a full-scale rehearsal in response to a perceived disaster must be carried out. Additionally, regular team meetings can and should take place. Funding is a priority. Contact your government officials to establish access. All members of the disaster response and resource (DRR) team will be clearly identified with badges, hats, T-shirts, armbands or whatever can be funded along these lines.

This plan is a guide to what could and perhaps should be put in place to cope with the aftermath of any disaster on Higatangan Island and others nearby. By the very nature of disasters, the response team will be presented with different challenges. Most importantly, some plan of action must be taken if the tragedy of Yolanda, or similar storms, is to be contained and dealt with in the future.

Contacts List: A comprehensive book of contacts must be compiled which include any perceived useful contacts, including: the DRR team, senators, members of congress, the local governor and mayor, all local officials, coastguard officers, air commanders, TV and radio stations, the naval hospital, Filipino and overseas aid agencies, and the government of the Philippines. In addition, the list of contacts may include any local residents who have relevant experience and knowledge, such as boat captains and boatman. Information is the lock, and teamwork is the key for such a plan to succeed.

International Rescue

I've already established that, internationally, the response to Yolanda would have made the Tracey Family and the Thunderbirds proud. It was an overwhelmingly humbling experience to be involved with as a private individual. The Americans led massive air lifts via helicopters that launched from aircraft carriers to complete field hospitals and transport heavy machinery, food, medical supplies, water, and personal hygiene products such as pallet loads of panties and toilet rolls. These items were sent along with a lot of money. Remember, in the United Kingdom, three pounds (about five US dollars) would buy a cup of coffee and maybe a biscuit. But in the Philippines, it's enough to feed a family of two adults and four children for a day, with a little bit leftover for sweets for the kids. The UK official estimate of government and private funding so far to the Philippines stands at the staggering 200 million pounds and counting. That's 1.4 billion pesos and rising. Imagine what you could achieve with that sum of money. My tiny island of Higatangan could be completely rebuilt with less than 1 per cent of that amount. Consider as well anonymous private sector contributions and from individual generosity. There were also high-profile donors such as Manny Pakyaw, the Filipino world champion boxer, who gave away millions of pesos. Yet two days after he regained his world title and gave the Filipinos a much needed moral boost, the Bureau of Internal Revenue (BIR) swooped down on him and demanded millions in unpaid taxes according to their claims. It's an ongoing battle, but surely someone as rich as Manny probably has a team of tax accountants dealing with his affairs. Surely the timing and the method of the BIR's accusation was highly questionable.

In my seaside hometown of Eastbourne, East Sussex, England, which has a population of around a quarter of a million people, fundraising was immediately instigated. I have a copy of some news articles from a local paper which could no doubt be duplicated throughout the world in many languages. The Eastbourne Filipino community, many of whom have no relatives in the disaster area, nevertheless sprang into action. Predictably, food came to mind, and I popped into the local Catholic school one Saturday afternoon. They put on a veritable feast of glorious grub for sale from which proceeds would go to the disaster aid fund. We don't have a particularly large community of Filipino in Eastbourne, but they came together even so. The same response was seen in thousands of similar communities throughout the world, and it formed an extremely powerful force. This should also serve as a not-so-friendly warning to all the venal politicians regarding the contempt for their people shown in their action or lack of it. One day, like so many of the rabid Filipino dogs, it will come back to bite them. When the next election appears on the horizon, with politicians who base their campaigns on lies and vote rigging, perhaps voters should avoid taking bribes and instead ask the candidates what they did to help in the aftermath of the worst typhoon seen in the Philippines. If you re-elect politicians who did nothing, I fear the senate building will be almost empty, and about six people will be running the whole country.

Images

One of the many enduring images I stumbled across on a social network captured the scene of a chain of Pinoys diligently unloading sacks of aid rice from an overloaded boat. In the middle of the slightly askew line, I saw a white woman in shorts and a T-shirt next to some Russian shot putters women. They were tossing fifty-kilogram bags of rice in unison with the Filipinos around them. I couldn't resist further investigation, which revealed that this lady and two of her friends had been in the Philippines when Yolanda arrived. They offered to help in whatever capacity they could, and their holiday adventure turned into an unforgettable experience. Well done, ladies! I wish I could say that welcoming committees of grateful Pinoys smoothed the path and gently helped these individuals who came to help them. I can't of course. In many cases, aid workers left their houses, families, jobs, and all the comforts of home to travel thousands of miles. I've met people who came from the United Kingdom, Belgium, France, Germany, Denmark, Norway, Sweden, Australia, New Zealand, India, Malaysia, Kuwait, Saudi Arabia, South Africa, and Tonga At the Cebu airbase, where I was fortunate enough to spend some time whilst aid distribution was martialled together by the US and Philippine Air Force, I also met a very confused and hot Icelandic man, a very long way from home. There was no excuse for me or my compatriots, who are possibly the laziest at learning languages, but English was spoken as a common language among all the relief workers. "Where shall we go?" and "What do you want us to do?" were the questions they asked most frequently.

Aid workers of varying levels came to the Philippines. Some were official government employees, including doctors, nurses, firefighters, aircrew, police military advisors and the inevitable civil servants and diplomats, many of whom were from the local embassy. The most important thing is that they came – national and international charities, big and small organizations, from the United Nations to an unpronounceable Swedish charity roughly translated as "Water for All." Yes, it quickly became "Waterfall." I gave up on correcting that pronunciation. The three workers from this organization were amongst the most delightful people I've ever met. Finally, members of NGOs and private individuals came to help. They probably never thought expected to encounter a visa scam in the Philippines. If these aid workers had the time and resources in their own country before they boarded the plane, the Philippine government – after much prevarication and mountain of paperwork – gave some sort of dispensation regarding visa requirements to these sterling individuals. But I have to tell you, I personally have never met anybody with this magical piece of paper. Everyone that I spoke to had the same horror story I did. They responded immediately and travelled, sometimes at their own cost, to the airport in

Cebu. Next, they queued up and prepared to travel to remote and devastated areas on paths that are not really roads, in boats that were not safe by any stretch of the imagination, and in a selection of other vehicles you would have to pay a scrapyard to take away.

Upon arrival, we were informed that additional visa rules applied unless you had paper sprinkled with fairy dust. After your first thirty days, on pain of death, you were required to return to an immigration office; they're located in Manila, Cebu, and, prior to Yolanda, Tacloban. I think that office is now floating somewhere in the China Sea. After thirty days, you fill out the form for a twenty-nine-day extension, pay money, fill out more forms, and apply for an ACR I-Card. Don't forget to dress smartly when you visit the immigration office; otherwise, the armed guard may shoot you. More than 10,000 pesos and, if you didn't pay the express fee, several hours later, you've received a small red stamp on your passport and a promised I-Card if you come back to collect it three weeks later. You may experience speechlessness, high blood pressure, and the thought, *Sod-it! I'll never do this again.* You shake your head as you hail a taxi to the nearest airport. And when you do leave the country, you have to pay an exit fee in Philippine pesos – no credit or debit cards accepted. It's a way to fleece visitors, and if you view it as such, you might not choose to pay. You don't have to stay here; come for twenty-nine days, and then go to another country – one that treats you as a valuable tourist, not a cash dispenser. Charging the people who came to the Philippines to help the country is utterly outrageous.

After I travelled to the remote island where my resort was located, which was devastated, I had to stop the work I was doing – not lying on the beach reading a book – and spend more than two days travelling to Cebu to renew said visa. Of course, my flight home added to the need for an extension. My arguments with the officials to add another ten days to make me NOT to come back were only accepted when I threw up my hands and threatened to take an early flight home, which would negate any visa extensions. Has anyone on the Philippine immigration team worked out yet that people can choose to travel many other places in the world? For example, I heard Vietnam is very relaxed about visas. I sincerely hope Yolanda's big sister doesn't visit the Philippines next year. If she does, I fear she will make the already hungry people starve as she whips away thousands of homes. People will suffer, and big-hearted aid workers will respond, but even more swiftly, we will be filling out forms, visiting the embassy, and arming ourselves with reams of papers to avoid paying money and wasting valuable time when we could be helping others.

Job Done in Cebu

By the time it was nearly Christmas, I knew I should be going to the island of Higatangan and the remains of the EBBR. I admit that I may have been putting it off because of the undoubtedly awful journey that awaited me and the knowledge that when I arrived, Yolanda would have left me a Christmas gift of chaos and an uncertain future. But in fear and trepidation, I set off. I would like to gloss over the journey and take you straight to the heart of it all on my totally destroyed beach. To do this, I would need to blag a helicopter, but the choppers were for aid relief distribution, not for transporting an Englishman because the boat and van journey made him sick as a dog. So, I had to make the endless journey from Cebu to the island by the traditional terrifying route. Leaving the comfort of my air-conditioned room, I went with my partner, Emily and her daughter, Emilys husband, and a female travelling companion, a sort of not really a maid The woman is over thirty-five, a mother of three teenagers, and her Pinoy husband buggered off twelve years ago. She is a very nice lady.

At four in the morning, when it was raining buckets of tropical rain, the taxi arrived almost on time to take us to the port of Cebu. Passengers and cargo mingled on the city's twenty-plus piers. It's fairly scary if all you've ever experienced is the cross-Channel ferry or boats to a cruise liner. We loaded the taxi to the gunwales with items such as soap, shampoo, toilet tissue, and panty liners for the ladies of the island. I managed to find some tea and a huge box of what they call corn flakes along with the bags of rice, noodles, canned goods, sugar, and – against my express wishes – a box of dried fish.

We arrived early – a word that I don't think translates into Filipino – because there was no traffic. We were pounced on by the obligatory dockside mafia porters, young and old, who rule with a rod of iron. They grab your bags, pile them precariously onto a creaking, squeaky trolley, and raise the load towards the boat. Count your bags, and make sure you head towards the right vessel; don't let them out of your sight for a millisecond. And if the porters don't lose your luggage, the lurkers might take it. They will have it away from you before you can say, "Take your hands off that bag, you shifty little fucker," drop all pretence of civilized behaviour, growl, stare, and shout! If you watch out for these risks, you might manage to board with your belongings intact. The porter will have, by then, conveniently forgotten the exorbitant price he quoted before loading his trolley, and now you have a fight on your hands, as that amount has tripled. Joy of joys, you have a winning hand. He has to get off the ship before it sails, and he loses the chance to rip off a few more poor sods whilst arguing with you. He ungraciously accepts the wad of notes to feed his family for a week and buy medicine for a non-existent sick grandmother and then shambles away, muttering. You slump down, exhausted, onto something that is probably not your bunk, as the porter left you in the worst possible location. It's next to the television blaring with a teenager and grinding music at full volume or near a family of with young children who cry and keep you awake all night. The ferry has various options, from economy, which offers a blanket and a plastic mattress on deck, to VIP room costing more than four times as much. I've tried them all except the VIP suite. On this trip, as I spotted the VIP room was empty, I thought I would give it a try. The following letter will answer what the experience was like.

> To Whom It May Concern:
>
> Which is probably no one at Roble Shipping. I have travelled frequently between Cebu and Naval on various Roble Shipping vessels, and I have been universally appalled at the level of service and hygiene provided. I've travelled economy, tourist, and cabin class. Finally, on Sunday 5 January 2014, I travelled from Naval to Cebu on the *Blessed Star* under Captain Gayle. I paid 2,000 peso for a VIP room. I was unaware that for Roble Shipping, this acronym stands for "very ignored person." The room was scruffy, with peeling wallpaper dirty floors and an even dirtier shower and toilet. For the entire voyage, there was no freshwater supply to shower, toilet, or hand basin. When a member of staff finally spoke to

me, I was dismissed with. The person said, "No water. Maybe later." I know that in the Philippines, that means never. The air conditioning was almost non-existent, so I was forced to abandon the room for the first few hours and sleep on the deck floor with just a blanket! The cooling system finally became effective three hours into the trip. There was no emergency torch and no door handles on the cabinet, and the toilet door complained more than I am now. It screeched loudly every time you had to force it open. There were no towels, no toilet seat, no tissue, and no rubbish bins.

Adding insult to injury, there was no hot water at the coffee bar. By the end of the trip, they had hot water but ran out of coffee for passengers. The crew seemed to have coffee though. I attempted to find someone on duty who wasn't asleep behind the counter. When I woke one and asked for the purser, no one seemed to know who that person was. I refused to leave the ship until I'd spoken to the purser, and that's all I did. He grunted and refused to give me the name of the captain, chief mate, or chief anybody. I was travelling with my Filipino partner, so translation was not a problem – just the attitude was. This was certainly not a VIP room or service. I was at the front of the queue of several complaining passengers from all sections of your boat. Your water bottle carries the slogan, "Bringing back the fun and joy of travel." Perhaps it should be changed to, "We have a virtual monopoly on these sea routes, so we don't care about you, the customer, at all." I would like a full refund but will accept a credit note, as I will have to use your service again. I'll go back to economy, I expect, as it's all the same – rubbish – unless, of course, I can find other foreigners to band together with to buy a boat and provide service sadly lacking from your company. The details of my ticket are: Name: Graham Barton; sailing date: 5 January 2014, receipt number 680195, VIP room. I have no expectation of a reply but would be very happy to receive one.

Yours in disgust,
Graham Barton

If enough people buy this book, I will be able to buy a ferry for the exclusive use of anyone prepared to pay a reasonable fare. This boat includes bathrooms with toilets that have a seat and flush; and you can turn on the tap and wash your hands. You will also get to sleep in a bed without cockroaches and escape noisy teenagers with mobile phones or portable media devices turning out constant music that drives you bleeding insane. The description of the diabolical journey doesn't bear repeating, so I will skip ahead to our arrival to the island. Note that the ferry doesn't go all the way to the island where the resort was. It docks to Naval, the nearest port, where you stand for hours unless you organize a boat to come get you.

The Official Response to the Disaster

How about the response from the military, the police, and the authorities? Ah, now that's a minefield. In fact, an actual minefield would be, in my opinion, less risky to negotiate through than the Pinoy authorities.

The following telling incident – one of many – is an example of what I mean. Some soldiers went AWOL during the actual typhoon event, but one young corporal returned to duty and reported to sort and distribute aid supplies. On finding out that his home village and his family were in the disaster zone, he requested and was granted leave of absence on compassionate grounds. Traveling on foot and by bus when there was one, he staggered under the weight of a backpack that any Special Air Service trooper would have been proud to carry.

When the man arrived at his mother's home, she was surprised and delighted to receive a veritable mountain of aid goods, nodding wisely at the purloined specialized medical packs. This type of aid distribution is an insignificant incident in the great scheme of things, but if you multiply it by millions of Filipinos, you've got serious problems. Much of the coverage on social media is directly from the Filipino people, and the people who stole from shops in Tacloban are called looters. Meanwhile, the people who continue stealing money donated to the people who wish to feed their families are called politicians.

Many such comments have appeared on the Internet, almost exclusively posted by compatriots. Perhaps the government hopes their history of general incompetence and inability to organize a piss up in a brewery will protect them from any revolutionary faction. However, this is not a constructive strategy even so. Now, I'm sure you won't wish to read a litany of what the authorities did – or in this instance did not – do after Typhoon Yolanda. It is, however, a short journey of discovery if I leave out the utter guff spewed by a collection of useless officials, politicians, and authority figures who should have responded to the plight of their people and were instead either incapable or culpable in a truly epic failure.

The cream that rose to the top amidst the circumstances was the Philippine Air Force. Now, I'm not party to the full military force of the Philippines but I was fortunate enough to meet a few of the helicopter pilots, the flight crews, and the flight coordinator. I would like to name these people in neon lights, yet knowing the Filipinos and the uneasy relationship between the military and the politicians as I do, I may not be doing them any favours.

On 9 November 2013, Super Typhoon Yolanda swept through a twenty-five-mile-wide stretch of the Pacific basin, and then concentrated its power on a group of islands in the middle of the 7,000. The storm cut a swathe affecting around 15 million people. Some were made homeless instantly, and others lost possessions. Even now, no one is quite sure how many lost their lives. Initially, the government made deliberately low estimates regarding loss of life. But when they realized they could get more sympathy and aid packages would kick in, they went for a figure above 10,000. Some might say, in other words, that the low figure was put out in ignorance, hoping the problem would go away, and the high figure was released when it dawned on authorities that there was money to be made.

Whatever the case, the international community showed an instant and phenomenal response, both in aid goods and money. When I met the pilots on the airbase, all of them volunteers, some were from Muslim and Catholic nations. The United Kingdom alone sent more than 3,000 people, along with ships, planes, goods, and money. This was an effective outpouring of actions and words, in that order. The ridiculous response from Filipino authorities was the reverse: their words spoke louder than their actions, apart from the Philippine Air Force efforts previously mentioned.

I have said it before, but it is worth repeating: If they'd channel the energy and effort they put into cheating, lying, and stealing into an honest, reasonable, fair distribution of aid goods and money, I probably wouldn't have enough material to put in this book. As it is, I have had to be selective in my recounting of corruption for fear of excess.

The Airbase

Please remember that this comes from my personal experience at the airbase and cannot be verified officially; I wouldn't want to put anybody on the spot. The political landscape in the Philippines is fragile. My experience with the officers, aircrew, police, and army within the airbase was all positive; the opposite has been true with politicians I've encountered. The only one I ever found honest and reliable, Glenn Chong, was forced from office, was cheated out of re-election, and emigrated to America in disgust. It was a loss – I'm sure – to the Pinoys. When I saw the following over a few days in the Cebu airbase, I was humbled, astounded, and horrified. I wish I could say these emotions were in equal measure, but the horror won out eventually.

The airbase in Cebu was quickly designated as the hub of distribution operations, and the Americans arrived in force just as quickly and took control of the apron – the airstrip to you and me. I had arrived at the perimeter gate dressed in standard trousers, a shirt, and a light jacket bearing a Union Jack patch on the breast pocket. The gate guard responded to my passport and hastily printed a card that said "Director of Higatangan Island Disaster Report Team" (it looks a bit like the logo of the Sussex police). I finished off by flashing the Hungarian police inspector badge, compliments of a grateful inspector I had assisted in my former life as a weapons expert.

I was in, and even better was the fact that the Pinoy military guard had upgraded me to a status of probably important. He called a police lieutenant who arrived with the coolest motorbike and sidecar, painted blue and white. I crouched in the cage, mesmerized; it was a shame she didn't use the siren, though.

Once I reached the apron, I was directed to the huge C-130 that had just landed and was taxiing to a halt. Unknowingly and fortuitously, I had arrived on the same day and time as one of several UK aid planes. It was an opportunity too good to miss; I fielded questions about what, where, and when and asked a few of my own. The delightful female lieutenant escorted me to the air co-ordinator's control room. Feigning innocence was not difficult, as I didn't actually know anything. I asked her to escort me, and she became my "get out of jail free" card for the next few days, bless her.

A sticky moment occurred at the very door of the control room. Two very alert, snowdrop-white helmeted Pinoy marine guards snapped to attention. I calmly saluted and pushed the door open. No one shot me, and my attention was drawn immediately to the huge wall map of the disaster area covered with red pins as I heard the buzz of conversation. Scanning the room, I saw pilots and aircrew of many nations: flamboyant French, chattering Italians, confused Norwegians, and a uniformed Pinoy.

As he turned, I caught his eye, and he came over to shake my hand. I had a folder stuffed with maps, letters, information, and anything that looked vaguely official, so I went into sales presentation mode. I knew that the first twenty seconds would set the tone, so I marched over to the map, tapped the speck that was Higatangan, and asked respectfully "Colonel, what can I do to get help to these people?'

He squinted at the speck and asked, "People here ... how many?"

I was in - the colonel was hooked and started firing questions at me. I could tell he was slightly miffed that he didn't know the island, but he was impressed that I, the perspiring Brit, had the answers, including map coordinates, a clear helicopter landing zone, beach fences located and clearly marked, a storage warehouse, the local officials under control, and a distribution team (Emily and the ladies from the village). There was no chaotic rushing to the helicopters as a few men with sticks kept order. I contacted Emily via text messages regarding the details of homes and people.

The colonel said, "I can't do a rice drop today, Mr Barton, but what do you want for tomorrow?" The man was a star. He sent me to the apron where I picked out goods. Water was not a priority, as wells were plentiful on the island. A lot of food, however, was needed. The international aid was stacked on the tarmac, and I chose noodles from Indonesia, canned goods from Australia, and a box full of premium goods and health products from the United States.

Aid Repackaging

I will add another telling and sad snapshot of the aid repackaging mentioned previously. One day, several ladies in Cebu arrived at a central distribution point under the Philippine authorities, where the US aid boxes had arrived. These boxes were crammed with supplies: canned goods of gigantic proportions, the best rice, and human-sized chocolate bars – enough to feed a family of six or eight for a week – and some treats many of the intended recipients had never seen before. God bless America.

The women were confused as to how they could help. All the towers of boxes were packed and stacked, ready for distribution.

Imagine their horror when they were shepherded to long trestle tables and instructed to open the boxes, take everything out, and stack it neatly in a growing mountain of glorious food.

The empty boxes were then repacked from another, less impressive mountain of shoddy local goods, canned rice, and small tins of so-called corned beef and canned ham product. When the boxes were half full, they were stuffed with plastic or paper and half-heartedly resealed. "Aid to the people" was scrawled on the outside. Much more could be said of this incident, but the fact that one lady spent a few hours repacking items with tears streaming down her face may be the most telling evidence. Several went home when they saw what was happening, and all confirmed that this is not an apocryphal story. It is probably just one of many stories that should bring shame and retribution on those who no doubt think they are getting away 'scot-free.

The mountain of goods from the United States was shipped off tout sweet to Manila and sold on the black market to greedy sari-sari (convenience) store owners, who sold the items at a profit. Don't forget – Yolanda never touched Manila, and residents there seemingly forget they are stealing from their own people.

Here is another revealing Facebook post from a Pinoy:

> Foreign relief packs, with portions for two people, contain: eight canned foods, eight packs noodles, two tins Spam, ten kilograms rice (Calrose – that's top quality), one gallon water, dried steak, chocolate bars, and some sweets.
>
> DSWD Pinoy authorities confiscate and repack in a bag with their logo on it. Now it contains two canned foods (local), one kilogram rice (local), and 350 millilitres water per family.

Is this streamlining, or is it simple corruption?

The Shopping Mall Experience

The shopping mall experience is not uniquely Filipino; these horrors infest most of the supposedly civilized world and are something not to thank the Yanks for. Pinoys love to shop, and their malls are jam-packed with electronic gizmo shops, supermarkets, and food halls, running the whole gamut of stuff that one wonders why the hell they need it.

I was quite shocked to find that only a few weeks after Yolanda wiped out a large slice of their country and its inhabitants that the people at the malls in Cebu seemed blissfully unaware of the suffering down the road. They only seemed interested in pizza with rice, Christmas toys, and more food. It was consumerism at its finest, or its worst – you decide.

Some cursory attempts were made to acknowledge the typhoon disaster, but most people carried on regardless. They accepted and absorbed the influx of refugees almost seamlessly and sort of knew someone who knew someone who had lost his or her home, possessions, and mobile phone to Yolanda. Are they inured to disaster, or do they not give a damn? What I can tell you is that the mushy sentiments expressed in religious hand-wringing and public protests broadcast via TV, radio, and social media sites have not been converted into any recognizable aid or assistance. These people might say, "If you lost your home in Tacloban, we're so very sorry, but I do really need a new pair of shiny shoes, and a Jollibee special with extra rice."

Whilst much of the shopping mall experience in the Philippines would be instantly recognizable worldwide, the security aspect isn't, and the service element leaves a lot to be desired. As you enter the mall, you are met by uniformed security guards festooned with Batman-style belts, usually containing empty pouches and holsters; occasionally there is a cursory medical pack, small baton, and a very suspect revolver (sometimes it's even loaded). However, whatever rests in the utility belt is rarely used. Security officers suffer through the low pay, long hours, lack of training, and on-the-job tedium as on any continent.

At the entrance of most malls, a table is positioned so that males go to one side; females, the other side. In practice, you might be patted down by a security officer of either sex, and sometimes a gloved hand with a small stick is poked aimlessly around in your bag – presumably looking for crazed bomb vests or suicide terrorists. As they lightly touch your hips and waist, the female guards have no idea the male shoppers enjoy it! And then you push into the heaving mass of humanity. You've kept your cap or hat on, nothing has been disturbed in your bag, and the small-but-deadly device you may have constructed from information on the Internet can be placed where it will do the most damage to the infrastructure and people. You see, security is not actually about protecting the shoppers – it's designed to stop them from nicking stuff. You passed the entrance test, but when you leave that's a different matter! Bags are peered at, and anything you've purchased has to be viewed and secured, usually in plastic bags with a little tie-up whatsit to close the bag in a knot that requires two strong men either side to pull it apart, thus destroying the bag. The receipt is taped to the outside of the bag. Boy, I wish I had the contract to supply the adhesive tape.

As you pass the logjam of the exit door, the guard has a stick with a red crayon attached, and he marks the receipt with it. The receipt gets several more red squiggles as you pass each floor, usually via an automatic stairway that hasn't worked for months. What joy it is to catch lazy, unsuspecting Pinoys gingerly take the first step and wait. Admittedly, the "Escalator Not Working" sign is askew and dust covered, but it still takes a build-up of bodies before the startling realization tinged with embarrassment hits them. Once they climb the staircase, a stream of humanity enters one of up to six or eight floors of stores. Boy, can the Pinoys shop!

These malls are, in the main, heaving. Whilst the shops seem to cater to the customer, the sales system is aggressive and counterproductive. At the top and bottom of staircase, a guard wields the ubiquitous red crayon. You don't have any other bags, as there is a bag storage counter on each floor. Any and all bags must be deposited with a couple of sloth-like teenagers who throw your purchases into a small hutch shelving unit and hand you a number. If you're very lucky when you return to the counter, reeling from the mall experience, you may even get the same belongings back. Just be firm that although the number on your ticket is for a hutch containing a bright-green handbag and a washing line, it is not what you (the middle-aged bloke from England) deposited.

Christmas Island

And so it was that in the season of goodwill towards all, I spent Christmas on the island. However, there was little sign of any will – good or bad – just sloth, as more than six weeks had passed since Yolanda hit, but international and local aid had failed to reach the island. Our singular attempts and those of other individuals working abroad or in other parts of the Philippines made significant inroads into the desperate needs of Higatangan. As I've written and Diana Ross sang, "I'm Still Waiting." Desperate needs aside, the population of the island and especially that of EBBR was determined not to get in the way of a good party.

The resort has the comparative luxury of access to our own generator. It is not enough to power the whole beach, but provides energy to several lights and, of course, the urgent necessity – the charging of mobile phones. There are also some small solar panels, and we brought some free-standing solar lights from Cebu. People panicked and dug up their buried treasure, borrowed from neighbours, and asked for a credit agreement with conditions worthy of mobile phone companies or the ones you forget to read when buying a widescreen telly. The saying "Gone in sixty seconds" springs to mind; everyone wanted to get some light at Christmas.

I feel I should make the religious connection here, but as an agnostic, I lack any credibility. The Catholic Church rules supreme on the island, with a sprinkling of other denominations. There are about eight churches on our tiny island of 3,000 souls, so when an act of God struck, I hoped our direct line to him via several ministries would provide a solution. However, I can't quite get a handle on what the church's response was to Yolanda. Some opened their doors to people made instantly homeless, and others provided immediate food and water, yet I feel their collective response was measured; a slight air of "we told you so" pervades. Nevertheless, religion reaped a reward from the whirlwind. Churches were packed for Christmas services, and the fear factor was at a premium. As I don't do or get the whole God thing, I can only observe. Whilst not lumping them all together with politicians, agencies, and others who failed to respond, I can't help the disquiet I feel when I see shell-shocked, needy people contributing and following the faith blindly. I'll make a final comment on this thorny issue – I trust you note the religious word choice, proving I have at least a working knowledge to make judgement upon, harking back to my spectacularly unprepossessing school reports, which read, "Graham is a disruptive influence in the class and must try harder." Replace "Graham" with "church," and you may concur my complaint.

The juxtaposition of the serious attention paid to God is the Filipino capacity to party, and Christmas provides the perfect opportunity. Because the island's inhabitants had survived Yolanda, there was a virtual certainty of feasting, dated dancing by dads, and – even worse – maudlin renditions of carols in English and the local dialect. Now, carolling presents a perfect excuse to fleece anyone foolish enough to let a disparate group, composed mainly of children, to band together and foist upon the listeners some truly awful carol singing. If they can't hold a tune or remember all the words in order, the fall-back position is shouting. They bang out a few verses and then shout, "Thank you, thank you!" until you give them some pesos to go away.

Lest you think of me as the Scrooge figure, this is not the end of my *Christmas Carol*. Over a five-day period, including Christmas Day, no less than forty groups, ranging from a quite impressive church group with guitars and a flute player to a couple of scrawny kids mumbling a few lines, appeared. My favourite one was a group of female teachers from the local school. They couldn't sing very well at all but looked extremely almost frightenly enthusiastic. .

Remember, at the end of the ordeal, you are obliged to pay. Multiply that by over forty visits, and it's a fair sum to pay to have your eardrums assaulted. Carollers may appear at any time and sidle up to where you are sitting on your balcony, reading a book on your e-reader and listening to proper music. Eventually, they form a sort of group, the bravest starts, and more by luck than judgement, they warble tunelessly until the time, mercifully, they finish. Even the pay-off is fraught with danger; give too little, and you are branded forever as a Scrooge; too much, and they rush off to tell their friends what a soft touch you are. Without doubt, each group contains a few familiar faces from previous visits. You get the feeling it's a planned campaign. You can fob off the smaller children with sweets alone, but the vast majority want hard cash –and a few sweets! If there were people on the island who practised other religions, certainly they would see this as an aggressive attack on their faith, as no one is spared the carollers.

I'll move on to discussing glorious food. Yolanda depleted the area's meagre food stocks, halting the supply to the local sari-sari stores. The cash flow dried up, banks closed, and traditionally at this festive time of year, remittances from family abroad run past the normal 45 to 50 per cent of GDP and spike as everyone tries to give their relations a happy Christmas. Western Union and other money changers and transfer companies were also affected by Yolanda and unable to operate. Restocking goods – not always easy at the best of times – becomes impossible. Perhaps the phrase, "Dried up after a storm surge," is inappropriate, but it's an accurate description. Fisher's boats were reduced to matchwood, so the natural source of food – the sea – was inaccessible. Three of the four pump boats (the small ferries used to access Naval, the nearest town) were damaged, and –the city of around 200,000 people had its own problems, as it was on a main supply route and relied heavily on Tacloban.

Hungry people became starving people, so Christmas grub was vital. By the time the holiday loomed, some order was back in place. Killing local pigs and chickens came high on the list when pulling out all the stops. Lechon baboy – the suckling pig – is a must. Chicken is a close second, and beef a last resort, as it's your investment. As Meat Loaf sang, "Two Out of Three Ain't Bad," so we got the drunk, one-eyed slaughter man to come to the beach at four in the morning to kill our prize pig while the lads strangled a few chickens. At dawn, the ladies began preparing all things edible and a few questionable straight-from-the sea, shell crustaceans, uncooked and disturbingly still pulsing quietly. By ten that morning, an impressive spread was ready, and a steady stream of hungry Pinoys came. We had harboured some of the aid goods, mainly hygiene products, and added some of our own foods brought in by boat: noodles and sweets for the kids, for example. The portions were so small but gratefully received. We handed out the presents. Precious fuel was used to power the video karaoke machine, so the day ended with traditional screeching and off-key singing.

The day after Christmas, 26 December, is known to we English as Boxing Day. There are several theories as to how the holiday was named. The boring one is that maybe not all boxes and packages would be cleared by this day. My preferred option is that in more genteel times, the lords and ladies paraded in their new finery, horses, and carriages received as gifts to a place to the south of London known as Box Hill. As a closet show-off, that's the explanation for me!

For the island Pinoys, Boxing Day consisted began by following someone not too drunk with a kerosene lamp back to a flattened nipa hut. Remarkably, the sounds of singing, shouted thank yous, laughing, giggling, and eventually snoring ended a not-so-bad Christmas on Higatangan.

Festival of Santa Niño Entertainment following Yolanda has been evenly spread between sparse and farce. Without electricity and with very little cash to purchase torches, lights, batteries, and in many cases food, all that is left is to party. During early January, there is always an island festival. It consists of two days of eating, drinking, dancing around handbags,as we all did in the 1980s at discos everywhere. Bad karaoke, occasional fights, kids dancing, and a Tsinela,shoe sale party – a sort of budget Rio Carnival. The word "Tsinelas" translates as "slippers". The festival is for Santa Niño (pun intended) – God only knows who he was, and who really cares? During the two days of partying, the usually shy Filipino ladies cavort in the streets wearing skimpy costumes. Forgive me if they all look suspiciously like bras and panties with shiny bits attached, as I'm not into fashion, but I still appreciate scantily clad ladies. It is a cursory competition, the winner of which gets, yes, a pair of slippers. As of now, no one has asked me to be a judge, but I have dropped broad hints that I'm open to non-financial bribes.

There were frantic preparations, as sound systems and disco equipment must come from other islands, and it is still storm season. The tennis court – on which I've never seen a tennis match – had a tarpaulin nearly secured over it. Small stalls sprang up everywhere, selling mainly food: barbecue, spicy anything on a stick, fried bananas, sticky rice, hot dogs, fish balls, and my favourite - chicken intestines. All are to be avoided by foreigners with weak stomachs. Drinks also arrived: crates of beer and versions of rum, brandy, and local firewater as well as crates of Sprite, Coke, and Fanta. There were also many small bags of rubbishy snacks and sweets. They were ready to party, and so the festival starts.

New Year's Day

New Year's Day 2014 on a totally damaged island in the middle of nowhere, celebrations were more removed from Trafalgar Square, London, or Times Square, New York City, than you can even begin to imagine. Starting in the early morning, a steady stream of people braved the hard rain in a motley collection of mismatched rainwear, and umbrellas that were broken, flimsy, or sported cartoon characters.

Grannies, kids, pregnant ladies, and more all arrived dripping and smiling to wish, "Happy New Year!" They really meant, "Can we have something from you?" We were prepared for the onslaught by repackaging sacks of rice into two-kilogram plastic bags, along with noodles, canned sardines, corned beef, and canned meat, plus a handful of sweets for the kids. It's uncomfortably too close to being feudal lords, but as we are the only ball game in town, accepting overly effusive thanks undermines my determination to name and shame the charlatans who talk a good game but leave it to a foreigner to help their constituents.

By five that evening, the cupboard in the warehouse is bare, but there is another delicious lechon baboy ready to eat. It has pride of place, surrounded by the traditional rice dishes, noodles, eggplant, dried fish, fish balls, and crates of drinks: beer, spirits, and Coke alongside the fearsome local brew, Balahina Tuba. Getting pissed quickly and cheaply is a foregone conclusion.

I apologize to the squeamish and the vegetarians, but this is life in the raw, as is the meat until cooked. The phrase "squealing like a stuck pig" comes wildly to life as you wake up to a cacophony of animals in their death throes. Mind you, the butcher works with alarmingly efficiency to dispatch, dismember, and dispense of inedible parts, and an army of local ladies with huge machetes starts the cooking process.

The makeshift tables groaned as the food piled up. By daybreak, initial inroads were made, but the real gorging didn't take place until the evening. This feast provided, on several levels, sustenance and the appearance of normality. It offered a celebration of survival, a sense of gathering around the table, a feeling of friendship, and most importantly, hope – in whatever form it took for each individual.

We had a full house – or the skeleton of one, and the weather was kind with some light rain and a gentle breeze. The day was spent primarily in food preparation and then eating. Strangely, on what is a family day in many countries, the children here arrive in ones and twos without adults. I believe they are gravitating towards where food, sweets, and potential presents will be. The visitors are seemingly random: some we know, and some we don't. They are noisy and excited as kids are everywhere.

The previous year here, we used the day to visit families across the island to give rice, noodles, tinned sardines, and sweets. It was fairly random. This year, target profiling seemed the order of the day because so many homes had been destroyed and families were beyond poor. We devised a simple system wherein we sent a couple of local staff members to identify the inhabitants whose homes and possessions were totally destroyed and gave them a ticket from an old raffle book. When those people made the trip to the beach, we exchanged the ticket for a bag of goodies. We managed to give almost 200 homes an eclectic mix of rice, noodles, canned goods, soap, and even panty liners. The steady stream of raffle winners took most of the day to come through, as there was talking and snacks to incorporate in the schedule. After this, the evening of talking, proper eating, drinking, loud music, and dancing beckoned. Our ancient generator heroically powered lights and my laptop for the use of iTunes. Andrea Bocelli and Italian opera had an uphill battle. Mozart, being dead, had no chance.

Thus ended two days of celebrations more poignant than previously, as we celebrated survival and the hope of a new beginning. Perhaps the traditional Christmas and New Year's precepts will ring true for these people in the Philippines. Whilst much is in their hands, much more is the responsibility of a higher authority – and I don't mean God. I am pointing directly at the government authorities, Christians, politicians, and individuals who, with a little effort and a little more humanity, can make next Christmas and New Year's Day very happy and prosperous for others.

Rebuilding

In the rebuild after the storm, of first importance was what they labelled 'the totally destroyed families. This is not a term for unstable relationships. It describes exactly what happened to their houses. I qualified too, as my beachfront cottage was amongst the first to go. Admittedly, I'd built it in the corner of resort, as far away from the locals as I could get and as close to the sea as possible for my daily swim, comfortably located next to the permanent resident (see chapter in *The very Small (Obviously) Book of the Philippines*).

It is a beautiful location with a view to die for. If I'd been there when Yolanda struck, I would have died. The ferocious typhoon spotted the silly foreigner's isolated home and totally destroyed it, first ripping away the roof, and then the walls, and finally the balcony. Try as she might, Yolanda couldn't dislodge the concreted-in European-size toilet, imported with a seat cover that bore a mawkish red telephone box and Houses of Parliament scene. There it sits, and so can I – a true public toilet, stalwart and obstinate, a testament to its owner.

Whilst I can claim to be part of the 40 per cent of the island that was totally damaged, I have the resources – well, a fairly meagre UK pension – to make a significant start in clearing and repairing the main rooms, replacing the resort cottages, and investing in a mountain of corrugated sheeting at local traders' vastly marked-up prices, as it's only that rich, stupid foreigner – the one who organized fundraising in the United Kingdom, purchased relief goods, delivered them to the island, diverted helicopters and international aid, and contacted charities, agencies, and even the office of the Philippine president. Perish the thought that I may sound a trifle bitter and twisted.

Returning to the nub of the matter – rebuilding –around 200 homes were destroyed. Therefore, the task for a lone Englishman and his small-but-determined Filipino partner was daunting, to say the least. The people are amazingly resilient and philosophical. They experience typhoons year in, year out, and let's face it, nepa hut materials and not-so-solid construction do not lend themselves to longevity or to resisting winds up to 200 miles per hour. So, rebuild takes money for tools, nails, and the roof.

At the time of this writing, two rooms and a toilet can be thrown up in a few days for around 300 US dollars or 350 Euros. So, it's do-able, but it isn't going to happen. All those generous donations from around the world and funds from governments, including that of the Philippines, could be used for this. My maths is not brilliant, but I calculate that to make life better, easier, and more profitable for your country as a whole, you could stop stealing and create some new programmes.

For example, using the aid money, you could set up an agency to buy everything needed to rebuild a simple home. With strong purchasing power, the materials could be secured at knock-down prices. Distribute the materials by road and sea, enlisting the help of the local people – especially the carpenters and labourers – to rebuild each home. There are charities already doing this and individuals trying to help, but imagine the tremendous power that a well-run, organized agency could achieve with a rolling programme of rebuilding each house, village, and island.

Yolanda was a disaster, but every cloud has a silver lining. In this case, homes that were shoddy and virtually uninhabitable were swept away, leaving the opportunity to rebuild a significant part of this country. What we, the international community, need to do now is to follow up on our generosity and press the Philippine government hard for details of where the aid goods and money went. Dig down into the much vaunted but unsubstantiated rebuilding programme simply, firmly, and while wearing the *Show Me the Money* hat.

It's of interest, I trust, to relate exactly how much cash and what materials it takes to rebuild a home for a family in the Philippines. Start first, as always, with the money: 200 pounds should do it; that's 300 Euros or 250 US dollars.. Six large sheets of plywood will make a shell for a large room and a sectioned-off kitchen area; it takes ten bags of cement mix for the flooring and two more for finishing cracks etc. You'll need twelve corrugated sheets and timber for the roof frame: six pieces of two-by-six and ten pieces of two-by-two. Finally, be sure to have four kilograms of nails, sizes one through three; you'll also need to pay for three days of labour – that's the basics. Of course, if you can add money for red oxide to keep the roof from rusting, paint for the plywood, plus luxuries such as sleeping mats, windows, and maybe an extra room, another fifty pounds should do it. This provides a family of four to six people with a home. In light of this, the spending money on other fabulous travel made me a bit uncomfortable. I'm not beating myself up and certainly not keeping score – nobody said life was fair. That said, I am pointing a finger at those huge organizations, especially the Philippine government, and reminding them that on a tiny island of 572 homes, of which a significant percent were damaged, the sum that was given, around half a million pounds, could, would, and must be found to rebuild Higatangan Island.

Juxtaposition of Circumstances

There is juxtaposition in my life as I write this chapter. I am sitting by an infinity pool atop a four-star hotel on Copacabana Beach, Rio de Janeiro, Brazil. I'm waiting for the world-famous Rio Carnival to start – five days of non-stop parties.

Now, why is a-middle aged fat bloke presently from the disaster-torn area in the Philippines not helping the people of the Philippines he is always banging on about? No excuses, but perhaps an explanation is in order. There is only so much one person can do to help those in need. Most of us make our contribution through donations, and it's a good thing we do. We recognize that you need an organization to get the best and swiftest results. Those of us who choose to help individually have to avoid running around like chickens with their heads cut off and suffer charity fatigue. We wake up one day and stare at the endless, immense task in front of us; if we happen to be in a bed, we then pull the covers up and hide. I have suffered this syndrome a few times. Guilt also tends to kick in after a while.

However, I have learned to separate my life into boxes, carefully closing one for a while and opening another. The box marked "Rio" was given to me by my grown-up sons – in my biased opinion, they are fine young men. As I had spent a lifetime dancing – disco, rock 'n' roll, salsa, and tango, following the maxim of dancing as if no one was watching – typical Dad dancing into my sixties presented no problem. As the big six-oh approached, I received a satellite phone call from my sons, who were in Antwerp and Shanghai, but being young had managed to set up a sort of conference call thingy. whilst I was in the bush, visiting a clinic I had set up in Gambia.

The call was to say, "Happy Birthday, old man. Our present to you is that we're taking you to the Rio Carnival in February 2014." I almost fell off the termite hill I was standing on. You see, if you are a Muslim, then a trip to Mecca is a must. As a dancer, Rio is the place to visit.

The Africans waiting in the queue for the clinic moved swiftly away from the dancing Englishman singing, "Oh boy, oh boy, I'm going to Rio!" I was deeply touched that my sons wanted to do this and slightly miffed they weren't sure I was up for it. The mind is willing, even if the knees are a bit weak. I said, "Book it, boys!" So, I am creaking quietly and loving every minute – even the ones when I have to give up dancing with dusky maidens and leave the lads in order to go sleep for a few hours.

Now, I include this part of the story to illustrate that an accident of birth and an opportunity to grow and prosper in a First World country is a fact of our privileged world. A small part of the shine is diminished by the stark knowledge that what I'm spending frivolously here in Brazil could do so much for a tiny island in the Philippines. I am not getting righteous or fanatical, and I am stealing all the soaps, shampoo, cotton buds, combs, and complimentary bags of peanuts I can get my hands on to take back from Rio, along with some new samba moves, for the ladies of Barton beach.

The Official Response to the Disaster AGAIN! No apologies dear reader for repeating this section ....it is the nub of this book,we can do what we can as individuals but the Authorities must take up the baton and run with it......NOW.

How about the response from the military, the police, and the authorities? Ah, now that's a minefield. In fact, an actual minefield would be, in my opinion, less risky to negotiate through than the Pinoy authorities.

The following telling incident – one of many – is an example of what I mean. Some soldiers went AWOL during the actual typhoon event, but one young corporal returned to duty and reported to sort and distribute aid supplies. On finding out that his home village and his family were in the disaster zone, he requested and was granted leave of absence on compassionate grounds. Traveling on foot and by bus when there was one, he staggered under the weight of a backpack that any Special Air Service trooper would have been proud to carry.

When the man arrived at his mother's home, she was surprised and delighted to receive a veritable mountain of aid goods, nodding wisely at the purloined specialized medical packs. This type of aid distribution is an insignificant incident in the great scheme of things, but if you multiply it by millions of Filipinos, you've got serious problems. Much of the coverage on social media is directly from the Filipino people, and the people who stole from shops in Tacodan are called looters. Meanwhile, the people who continue stealing money donated to the people who wish to feed their families are called politicians.

Many such comments have appeared on the Internet, almost exclusively posted by compatriots. Perhaps the government hopes their history of general incompetence and inability to organize a piss up in a brewery will protect them from any revolutionary faction. However, this is not a constructive strategy even so. Now, I'm sure you won't wish to read a litany of what the authorities did – or in this instance did not – do after Typhoon Yolanda. It is, however, a short journey of discovery if I leave out the utter guff spewed by a collection of useless officials, politicians, and authority figures who should have responded to the plight of their people and were instead either incapable or culpable in a truly epic failure.

The cream that rose to the top amidst the circumstances was the Philippine Air Force. Now, I'm not party to the full military force of the Philippines but I was fortunate enough to meet a few of the helicopter pilots, the flight crews, and the flight coordinator. I would like to name these people in neon lights, yet knowing the Filipinos and the uneasy relationship between the military and the politicians as I do, I may not be doing them any favours.

On 9 November 2013, Super Typhoon Yolanda swept through a twenty-five-mile-wide stretch of the Pacific basin, and then concentrated its power on a group of islands in the middle of the 7,000. The storm cut a swathe affecting around 15 million people. Some were made homeless instantly, and others lost possessions. Even now, no one is quite sure how many lost their lives. Initially, the government made deliberately low estimates regarding loss of life. But when they realized they could get more sympathy and aid packages would kick in, they went for a figure above 10,000. Some might say, in other words, that the low figure was put out in ignorance, hoping the problem would go away, and the high figure was released when it dawned on authorities that there was money to be made.

Whatever the case, the international community showed an instant and phenomenal response, both in aid goods and money. When I met the pilots on the airbase, all of them volunteers, some were from Muslim and Catholic nations. The United Kingdom alone sent more than 3,000 people, along with ships, planes, goods, and money. This was an effective outpouring of actions and words, in that order. The ridiculous response from Filipino authorities was the reverse: their words spoke louder than their actions, apart from the Philippine Air Force efforts previously mentioned.

I have said it before, but it is worth repeating: If they'd channel the energy and effort they put into cheating, lying, and stealing into an honest, reasonable, fair distribution of aid goods and money, I probably wouldn't have enough material to put in this book. As it is, I have had to be selective in my recounting of corruption for fear of excess.

Three Months and Counting

It has been three months since Yolanda paid us a visit. The local barangay hall (town council), the body responsible for the island that is based in the city of Naval, has issued tickets to a few of the homes in Higatangan that were considered totally destroyed. There was much excitement on our island, as the matriarchs of the forty families banded together in a chattering group and set off at the crack of dawn to take the ferry and queue noisily but determinedly outside the Naval county hall. It should be no surprise that lots of forms must be filled out to get a result. Here's an example for you: a lady with three kids and an elderly mum staying with her, after her husband buggered off to Manila while she was a pregnant, expectantly handed in the ticket, filled out the forms, and is given 1,000 pesos; that's around 15 pounds or 20 US dollars. It is hardly enough to build a shelter for hobbits and will buy only a couple of sheets of hardboard and perhaps even a small door. This is not a rebuilding program; it's an insult to all. The message is, "See, we are helping people rebuild. Vote for us in the next election because we gave you 1,000 pesos – once we had our share, of course." In layman's terms, they were just taking a piss.

Yes, there were millions affected, but billions in pesos were donated, and this woman's house could be rebuilt for around 250 pounds or 350 dollars. On Higatangan Island around forty homes are totally damaged. That means it would take around 50,000 pounds or 75,000 dollars to get them shelter. So, dear reader, how much did your country give, and where did that generosity go? The United Kingdom gave over 200 million pounds (equivalent to 1.5 billion pesos). Therefore, 50,000 pounds is such a small fraction of the amount that was donated. I know it's a small island, and many need help, but even Tacloban has received a significant amount of funds, mainly for government buildings, Oh yes, the immigration office was up and running a couple of weeks after the disaster, but much of the aid was wasted; as soon as the typhoon hit, everybody left. Whilst I was in Cebu at the airbase, thick crowds of refugees quickly arrived. As the aid poured in to the damaged airport and the broken seaport, the people poured out. A different sort of disaster was inevitable: the disaster of disorganized corrupt chaos. The mayor of Tacloban made a desperate plea for people to return. It was hard to get funds and goods without people. The chaotic conditions attracted the portion of society only too willing to snatch freebees and aid goods. Let's not forget the hundreds of prisoners inadvertently freed, compliments of Yolanda. Shortly after the typhoon, Tacloban become a ghost town. The road into the city – and there was only one open – was incredibly dangerous. There were fallen trees, poles, holes, and debris on the highway as well as bandits everywhere. The only way into the empty city was in a van full of armed police returning to duty. Annoyingly, the English weapons expert was only given a stick; it didn't even look like a gun!

What's Next?

So, what of the future? Well, there will be no more books from me about the Philippines, but I may stretch out my retirement into a whole new future as a writer.

The future of the Philippines is uncertain. Whilst Super Typhoon Yolanda has gone, her children will visit these islands on a regular basis. The alphabetical typhoon season will bring wind, rain, destruction, and misery. The Pinoys won't be prepared or surprised. I've done my bit in trying to assist, partially through the action plan outlined earlier in this book. They'll need to undergo a few more disasters before it's considered or, perish the thought, implemented. They liked the badges and armbands, though! The government could shape up, tackle corruption, and use funds generously given to rebuild their shattered country. If they put in place responses to future disasters that are effective, the happy people on the islands will have a future to be proud of. The reality is, "There go those flying pigs," which will promptly be roasted on a spit and served with rice if caught.

Tacloban

Endless tales of corruption, greed, inefficiency, and avarice are frankly tedious and depressing –for me to write and for you to read. Each day brings more chapters – rarely uplifting – but here's one final story.

The city of Tacloban took the brunt of the typhoon and, owing to totally inadequate defences, suffered a storm surge that was actually a mini tsunami. In minutes, it was wiped off the map. The airport vanished, and the harbour, dockside, and town centre were demolished. There was tragic loss of life and damage on an apocalyptic scale. The world responded, and aid poured in, but the city didn't see much of it.

Almost a year on, I fought my way to Tacloban on what was still the only road into the city. The shining vista of a spectacular new city greeted me, and then I awoke from my dream in the bone-shaking van as it screeched to a halt in a rubble-filled parking plot. Nothing except government buildings had been repaired – Tacloban was still a mess.

I walked cautiously, picking my way through the rubble and nodding to squatting Pinoys in their half-built or half-destroyed homes, until I arrived at the remains of the town centre.

Typhoon Yolanda had furiously swept up a couple of huge ships – two steel tankers of considerable tonnage. One was deposited over the area of two or three main shopping areas, and the other joined a party through the complete area of a McDonalds building, coming to rest as a unique take on a drive-through.

A year after the tropical cyclone, the rusting hulk was in the process of being cut up and removed. I suspect Ronald McDonald and his money were instrumental, as dozens of workers with oxyacetylene torches and numerous tools swarmed over the superstructure.

Further down the road, ship number two – a substantial three-decker – was still in situ after falling, but Philippine ingenuity turned it into a residence; about one hundred families have made this tanker their home. There are ladders everywhere, and children play on deck; galleys are kitchens, and engines provide power. It's a regular SS *Home Sweet Home:* a trifle noisy and somewhat smelly, yet there it is – the power of people at work. No doubt, at some time in the future, the Philippine government will work out there's money to be had from salvage and eject the families to be rehoused in brand new homes paid for by the money from the international community. I made that bit up, but let's just say good luck to all on board the SS *Home Sweet Home!*

A Friendly Warning

When asked if it was possible to make a small fortune in the Philippines, I replied, "Why yes, of course. Just bring a large fortune, and in a few short weeks, the Pinoys will turn it into a small one."

Whilst a visit to these islands is recommended, please don't be disappointed. All your foreign aid hasn't achieved anything. If you wish to find a positive amidst the circumstances, the next time some unspeakable disaster unfolds in front of your eyes in a far-flung land, you may take a moment and reflect that perhaps charity really does begin at home.

About the Author

Graham Michael Barton, the Englishman in question, stayed in school to about the age of fifteen. He was expelled and considered a bad boy, with no qualifications and a learning curve that had gone steeply downhill from the age of ten. His patient-but-mystified father sent him to an Army Apprentices College location, where his older brother had excelled. Unsurprisingly, in less than six months, Graham was again discharged as a bad boy. Graham's dad refused to tolerate his son's singular lack of enthusiasm for education and insisted he find work. As jobs were plentiful back then, the uneducated, unqualified, slightly angry, and frustrated young man started working in a frozen-food factory. He moved swiftly to a rope factory, became a furniture salesman, worked in a supermarket, and had a spell as an ice-cream salesman. All this was before the age of twenty.

Graham soon realized that to make serious money, he had to work for himself, and he chose his hobby of martial arts, where fighting and winning gave cash prices. But winning wasn't a given. Losing fights in spectacular fashion gave him the time and opportunity to sell specialized products to his fellow martial artists. Many asked him to find particular weapons, and he sourced these from manufacturers in Spain and Europe. From his one-room flat above his family's taxi office, Graham sold Japanese swords, martial arts equipment, replica guns and knives, and militaria. Then film companies producing movies such as *Shogun*, *Enter the Dragon*, and the James Bond series recognized Graham as the supplier of all things weapon-related. As the years passed, orders from many other film productions including *Gladiator* and the *Lord of the Rings* movies took his business, Battle Orders Ltd., to number one in this admittedly limited field.

During this time, Graham travelled to the Philippines to have products manufactured to his design. Emily Poyos, Graham's business partner and a naturalized Filipino, advised him on one such trip to buy land there. Over the years, they developed Emponet Barton Beach Resort, where Graham retired a few short months before Typhoon Yolanda interrupted his plans. His book *The Very Small (Obviously) Book of the Philippines* reflects his unique experiences in the Philippines. This book, his second, contains his observations on what happen after the super typhoon Haiyan (Yolanda) visited the Philippines. Graham promises that this is his last book about the Philippines, but if enough people buy copies of the first two books, he may be able to write something else equally entertaining. Those of you who have been to the Philippines will recognize the phrase, "It's up to you!"

About the Book

Graham Michael Barton is an Englishman retired on a tiny island of less than three thousand souls in the Philippines. Emponet Barton Beach Resort and 60 per cent of the homes on Higatangan Island, Biliran, were destroyed by Yolanda. Two weeks after the super typhoon passed through, Graham returned with a modest amount of supplies and food, distributed throughout the island by his partner, EmilyPoyos, who had been born there. The devastation was so severe that Graham returned to Cebu to organize helicopter air lifts and do whatever he could to get aid to his adopted island and its people. During this time, the international community responded magnificently, and Graham had the opportunity to visit the airbase at which most of the aid supplies arrived.

This book contains his account of those days and the subsequent hunt for where the aid and billions of pesos went. None of it arrived on his small island. His queries about where the money went were rebuffed.

Graham freely admits that he is only one person, and he fervently hopes many more are demanding, "Show me the money!" His first book, *The very Small (Obviously) Book of the Philippines*, is a series of snapshots of his experiences as a foreigner in the Philippines. I hope that some found it amusing and entertaining. *Show Me the Money*, dear readers, is not very funny at all.

This book is dedicated to the PHILIPPINE AIRFORCE. Without whom aid would have sat on the tarmac...... risking their lives for their own people was,in their words, absolutely the right thing to do.

Lightning Source UK Ltd.
Milton Keynes UK
UKOW05f1135041114

241080UK00001B/5/P